CW00493550

A LINCOLNSHIRE RAILWAY CENTRE

A. J. LUDLAM

Published by the
Lincolnshire Wolds Railway Society

Immingham shed's giant concrete coaling plant. Known as the 'Cenotaph', it still stands today as a reminder of the days of steam.

Immingham Dock in 1963. The dock entrance is in the bottom left-hand corner with the graving dock to the right. Just two coal hoists remain in place. The variety of ships is indicative of the different cargo being traded in the days before super-tankers and container ships came to dominate the sea lanes of the world.

ISBN 978-0-9954610-0-0

The Lincolnshire Wolds Railway Society would like to thank Alf Ludlam and Phil Eldridge for giving their time to compile this publication, to Immingham Museum, Leyland Penn, David Enefer and William Gladwell for their contributions, and to Allinson Print & Supplies for their support with the project.

Printed by Allinson Print & Supplies, Allinson House, Lincoln Way, Fairfield Industrial Estate, Louth, Lincolnshire LN11 0LS

Issue 1. Summer 2016.

CONTENTS

**A 1927 view of Immingham shed in its original form.
The engines reflect its GCR heritage.**

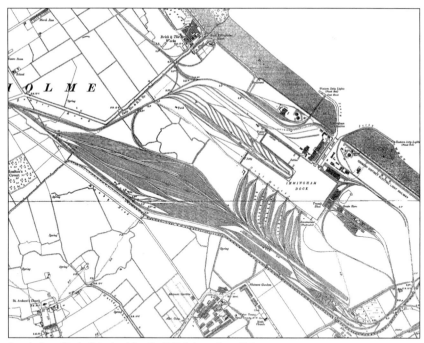

Immingham Dock. *Reproduced from the 1932 Ordnance Survey Map.*

The Coal Hoists. *Grimsby Library*

INTRODUCTION

It was the twentieth century that made Immingham what it is - a port with a deep-water dock, and a land-locked harbour, entered by a deep-water channel through which the largest trading vessels can pass.

The village, two miles inland, grew with the coming of the dock. The church has a 15th century tower, but the north arcade of the nave was built at the close of the Norman period. On one side of the chancel hangs the White Ensign and on the other the Stars and Stripes, given by American sailors who were at Immingham during World War 2.

A granite monument on the Humber shore recalls a little ship and a few people who faced the unknown more than four centuries ago. The little creek near the monument was the place from where the Pilgrim Fathers set sail for Holland in 1609 in search of religious freedom. Eleven years later they sailed across the Atlantic, a voyage that led to the foundation of the United States of America.

From the end of the 1840s the town of Grimsby occupied a leading position in the league of railway ports. With the arrival of the Manchester, Sheffield & Lincolnshire Railway (MS&LR) it developed from a small fishing village into the world's premier fishing port. At the same time it became an important trading centre for timber, coal and general merchandise. As coal traffic increased the docks diminishing capacity to deal with it was giving cause for concern. After some debate the directors of the Great Central Railway (GCR), which had succeeded the MS&LR in 1897, decided to build a new port to relieve the pressure on Grimsby. It was to be sited six miles upstream from Grimsby on the River Humber, the intention was to complement, rather than replace, Grimsby.

The tiny village of Immingham was chosen as the site of the new dock. The ceremonial first sod was cut by Lady Henderson, the wife of the GCR chairman, Sir Alexander Henderson, on 12th July, 1906.

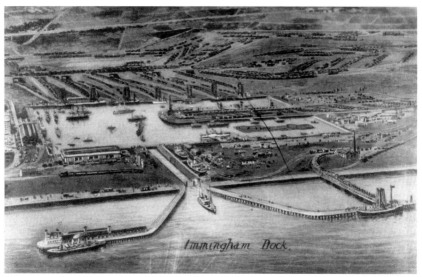

A birds-eye view of Immingham. On the far side of the basin are the coal hoists and the lines that served them, Western and Eastern jetties jut out into the River Humber in the forground.

ENGLAND'S LATEST PORT
IMMINGHAM
(Grimsby)
DEEP WATER DOCK

VIEW OF COAL HOISTS CAPABLE OF SHIPPING 5,000 TONS PER HOUR.
Accommodation for 11,600 Loaded Wagons, 170 Miles of Sidings
AVAILABLE FOR THE LARGEST SHIPS AT ALL TIDES
For information apply to GREAT CENTRAL GOODS AGENTS or PORT MASTER, IMMINGHAM DOCK, GRIMSBY

2

BUILDING OF THE DOCK

The contract for building the dock was awarded to Price, Wills & Reeves, under the supervision of Robert Hollowday. During the construction 1,000 miles of temporary track, 30 locomotives, 1,416 wagons, 10 steam navvies, 39 cranes, 39 pumps, 26 boilers, 30 horses and 14 pile drivers were employed. There were 2,500 men working on the site, 600 of whom were transported daily from Grimsby by the "Navvy Mail", made-up, not of the customary open wagons, but of old Metropolitan Railway passenger stock.

A few miles from Immingham, at Brocklesby, the contractors bought and worked a stone quarry. This provided the essential stone for the huge quantities of concrete and ballasting that the project consumed. Close to where the docks were being excavated a workshop was built where anything from a tip-wagon to a locomotive could be made and repairs to equipment and plant be carried out.

Granite, used in the copings and lock quoins, was shipped from Sweden, while timber (jarrah, pitch pine, elm and oak) was delivered from Russia, America and Australia. Gravel came from Sunderland and the south coast of England. Some 50,000 tons of cement were moved by barge from the River Medway. 320,000 cubic yards of concrete were used together with 30,000 cubic yards of brickwork. At the entrance jetties the river channel was dredged for a considerable distance, with an estimated 1.5 million cubic yards of mud removed and pumped through 24in diameter wrought iron tubes onto the land. This, plus the 3,500,000 cubic yards excavated from the dock, raised the dock site by almost 5 feet.

The dock area covered approximately $2\frac{1}{2}$ square miles and the frontage on the southern bank of the Humber was $1\frac{1}{2}$ miles in length. Among the advantages of the new dock complex were the deep-water jetties. Here the largest ships could tie up and land or embark passengers and perishable cargoes, or take in bunker coal without entering the dock. Cranes were provided, along with massive warehouse and storage facilities. Upwards of 170 miles of sidings were linked to the coal hoists, transit sheds, granaries and other buildings. An incentive to use the dock was the setting of Pilotage and Conservancy fees at rates lower than any other dock on the Humber. A graving dock, which ships could access with ease, was also provided. General charges to ship owners were less than elsewhere and there was no tedious use of tenders for passengers. Similarly, there was no hindrance to direct transhipment from ship to rail and vice-versa.

Immingham Dock had an entrance lock 840ft long and 90ft wide. The southwest arm measured 1,250ft x 375ft and a timber pond of 6 acres was located in the northwest arm. The water area, including the timber pond, was about 45 acres. The entrance lock was constructed on ample lines, with a depth over the sill at high water of 47ft, while at low-water the clearance was at least 27ft and therefore able to admit any vessel likely to trade along the east coast.

The lock entrance gates were massively constructed with each of the outer gates no less than 56ft 6ins high x 53ft 6ins wide. The middle gates were 54ft 6ins high x 53ft 6ins wide, while the inner pair were 42ft 6ins high x 53ft 6ins wide. The depth of water in the dock ranged from 30ft to 35ft and was able to accommodate the largest ships afloat. Two long curved jetties emerged from the sides of the entrance lock and were linked by double-track to the railway system of the docks. The Eastern Jetty was reserved for passenger traffic and had its own station. On Western Jetty a hoist was erected for the shipment of bunker coal.

Views of the 'Wild West', some of the temporary shops that were erected for the use of the construction workers who were building the dock.

The graving dock on the left and the dock offices on the eastern side of the entrance lock with the Western and Eastern jetties beyond. This and the image below are featured in the June 1912 edition of The Railway Magazine.

A heavy cargo crane at work at Immingham Dock with the dock offices and the two jetties beyond.

MS&LR locomotive 2-4-0 No 79 was built in 1849 as 'Acteon' and was rebuilt in 1886 to this condition. It had 18in x 26in cylinders, 6ft 9in coupled wheels and was scrapped in 1902. It is seen here at Oxbrow Crossing, New Holland in the 1890s.

Western coaling jetty with an independent coaling hoist for bunkering vessels at any state of the tide.

6

The impressive grain elevator at Immingham Dock which stood on the east side of the dock basin and was equipped with an elevator and automatic weighing machines. Railway tracks ran along the front and rear of the building in the foreground. This image also featured in the June 1912 edition of The Railway Magazine.

A boat train meets a liner at Eastern Jetty, Immingham in the 1920s.

Class D9 4-4-0 No 6024 stands in the middle road at New Holland Pier station awaiting the arrival of a train from Cleethorpes. Built in 1902 No 6024 was transferred from New Holland in 1935 and was withdrawn in 1949. New Holland Pier Head station was a bleak place particularly during wet and windy conditions.

Class N5 0-6-2T No 69305 waits in the platform at Barton on Humber station with a train for New Holland on 28th April, 1954. None of the station buildings survive today. *H. C. Casserley.*

COAL AND TIMBER

Seven coal hoists stood in a row on the south side of the large basin. Each hoist was served by a full set of sidings tapering to a single line near the hoist. Loaded wagons were run onto the hoist, lifted and tipped by hydraulic machinery. The empty wagons were brought to the level of an overhead gantry, from where they descended by gravity on a second set of rails to empty sidings. Each hoist was capable of delivering 700 tons of coal per hour, or 5,600 tons when all the hoists were working to capacity. One of the hoists was moveable, thereby making it possible to work two holds of a ship simultaneously.

There were eight gravity sidings connected to each hoist, each of them capable of holding forty 10-ton wagons - 320 wagons per hoist. In the storage and reception sidings nearby there was room for 9,120 wagons.

Adjoining the timber pond was a yard where timber could be stacked. Five 30 cwt cranes dealt with the handling and sorting of timber shipments. A huge granary was built at the east end of the dock, with an elevator and automatic weighing machines.

A train for Immingham at Killingholme Admiralty Platform on 28th April, 1954.

Ex-NER class J21 0-6-0 No 289 stands alongside the coaling stage at New Holland shed in 1932. This engine and another of the same class spent nine months at New Holland during this time. In 1912 Immingham took over maintenance work formerly carried out at New Holland, the latter becoming an outstation for Immingham-based engines. New Holland shed officially closed in 1938, but continued to function for many years afterwards.

Class N5 0-6-2T No 69305 takes water at New Holland shed in June 1952.

THE POWERHOUSE

A powerhouse was built close to the Western Jetty, which supplied hydraulic power for all the machinery, as well as electricity to illuminate the dock areas both at Immingham and Grimsby. The electrical equipment at Immingham ranged from lighting and traction on the Grimsby & Immingham Electric Railway (G&IER) to pumping in cooperation with the hydraulic department. The graving dock was a good example of the use of electric power for pumping. The basin held 1,215,000 cubic feet of water and the pump could empty the dock in 84 minutes.

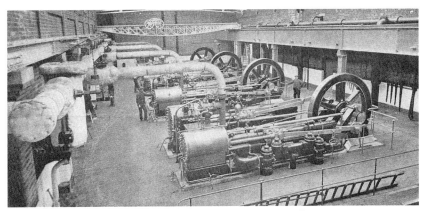

Hydraulic engines in the Immingham Dock Power House. *The Railway Magazine*

A battery of nine Lancashire boilers in Immingham Dock Power Station. *The Railway Magazine*

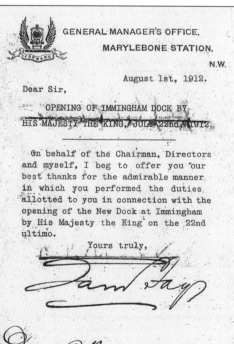

Above:
Grimsby Stationmaster Tom Jervis seated left on the platform edge of the garlanded station. With him the extra police drafted in for the arrival of HM King George V and Queen Mary on the day the King opened Immingham Dock, Monday 22 July, 1912.

Left:
A letter from Sir Sam Fay, General Manager of the Great Central Railway, to Driver Parkinson of Grimsby, thanking him for his duties performed during the official opening of Immingham Dock.

Right:
The paddle steamer "Killingholme" arrived at Immingham Dock with HM George V and Queen Mary on board for the opening ceremony. Waiting alongside No 2 transit shed is the official GCR delegation. *Grimsby Library*

THE OPENING OF THE DOCK

After six years of construction work Immingham Dock was officially opened by HM King George V, on 22nd July, 1912, although, due to urgent requirements of the coal industry, the new dock was brought into partial use on 15th May. The GCR ran special trains from London and Manchester and local people were carried over the Grimsby District Light Railway and the electric railway.

At Grimsby Town station the King and Queen Mary were welcomed by the GCR chairman, Sir Alexander Henderson and Sam Fay, the General Manager. The Royal Party left Grimsby Dock station behind 4-4-2 locomotive No 364: "Lady Henderson", one of John Robinson's magnificent Compound Atlantics. The train arrived at a specially constructed platform opposite the locks at 2.20 pm. Boarding the paddle steamer "Killingholme" the King and Queen travelled through the locks and made a circuit of the dock before coming ashore alongside No 2 transit shed. Here Sir Alexander Henderson made a short speech, during which he asked permission to name the new dock "Kings Dock". The King agreed to the request and declared the dock open. To everyone's surprise Sam Fay was summoned to the dais where the King bestowed a knighthood upon him.

Class A5 4-6-2T at Immingham Dock station in June 1952 with a train of interesting coaching stock.

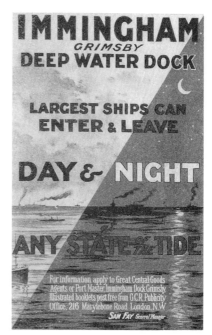

RAILWAYS SERVING THE DOCK

The new dock was served by three railways. Firstly there was the Grimsby District Light Railway, which opened in May 1906 and was used by trains conveying materials during the building of the dock and by dock employees. It was realised that the public could well benefit from the line, so, from 3rd January, 1910, a steam rail motor service operated, departing from a wooden platform at Pyewipe. Fares were 6d, with workmen paying 4d. The line was also used to transfer engines to and from the newly opened Immingham locomotive depot to Grimsby and its docks. The passenger service ceased with the opening of the Grimsby & Immingham Electric Railway in 1912.

Robinson introduced the seven distinctive **GCR** class 5A 0-6-0Ts between 1906 and 1914 specifically to dock sidings at Immingham and Grimsby. Here we see **No 157** as BR **No 68207** at Immingham shed on 19th May, 1952. *H. C. Casserley*

Gateshead car No 26 (left) stands alongside ex-GCR car No 1 at Immingham in the 1950s.

Grimsby & Immingham GCR car No 4 works along Gilbey Road followed by a Grimsby Transport motor bus. *A. D. Packer*

16

THE CLICKETY

This was perhaps the best-known railway running into Immingham and was affectionately known as "The Clickety". Sanctioned under the Grimsby District Light Railway order of 1906, it was built alongside the Light Railway on the landward side, between Immingham and Pyewipe. From here the track entered Grimsby running along Gilbey Road and Corporation Road to a terminus at Corporation Bridge. The country section was built by Price, Wills & Reeves, the street section by R. W. Blackwell & Co, who also supplied the overhead wiring.

Originally it had been intended to only construct the street section, which would connect with the steam rail motors running on the Light Railway. The decision to continue the line through to Immingham was taken on the basis that electric traction was preferred to steam because it was deemed more convenient for the 24 hour operation that the tramway provided. This round-the-clock operation was linked to Immingham engine shed and its need to roster crews and shed staff at all hours of the day and night. Similarly dockworkers at Immingham had to be able to get to work at all hours. The line opened on 15th May, 1912 with the 5 mile run taking 20 minutes.

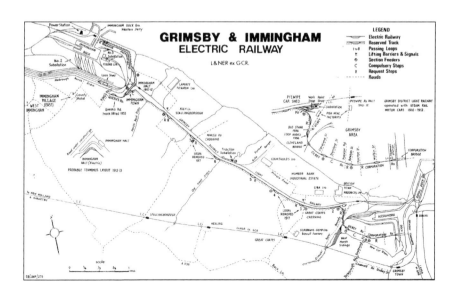

There were originally sixteen single-deck double-bogie tramcars. Nos 1-4 and 9-16 had 50 hp motors and seated 60 passengers, whilst Nos 5-8 were of similar appearance but had 30 hp motors and seated 40 passengers. Tramcars 6-8 were scrapped in 1931 and No 5 became a works car. Thirteen of the original GCR cars were taken over by British Railways in 1948. These were augmented by three ex-Newcastle cars, Nos 29, 77 and 45, which were numbered 6-8. They were not successful and were replaced by eighteen ex-Gateshead cars in 1951, which became Nos 17-34.

In June 1956 Grimsby Corporation exercised rights provided for in the 1906 Light Railway Order, to purchase the section of track within its boundaries. Operations between Corporation Bridge and Pyewipe ceased, but the tramway continued to run for another five years. The end came on Saturday 1st July, 1961, when dozens of people turned out to bid farewell to the trams.

A good view of the bridge over the Alexandra Dock, Grimsby behind car Nos 3 and 15 at the terminus station on 15th October, 1955. *I. Wright*

HUMBER COMMERCIAL RAILWAY

This was Immingham's most important rail link. It connected the port with the rest of the GCR system and, through that, the country at large. The line joined the Grimsby-New Holland line immediately north of Ulceby station. From here it ran eastwards 3½ miles to Humber Road Junction, where it divided, with one set of rails running along the south side of the dock estate, providing access to the coal hoists and marshalling yards. It then passed the locomotive depot to join the Grimsby District Light Railway at the triangular Immingham East Junction. From here the line headed north, then west to run alongside the river before arriving at Eastern Jetty. The other set of tracks carried on northwards from Humber Road Junction and then turned east, providing access to Western Jetty and terminating at Immingham Dock station. The 8¼ mile double-track line opened for contractors in January 1910 and was fully completed in May 1912.

The contractor used no less than thirty locomotives during the construction of Immingham Docks, and we see here one of the narrow-gauge engines, Kerr Stuart 0-4-2T 'Beaufort'. The driver, John Thomas, has posed with his fireman so that the photographer could record them at work for posterity. In the background can be seen some of the temporary buildings erected while construction was underway.

GCR class 6B 4-4-0 No 439 with a New Holland bound passenger train at Immingham Dock station.
E. B. Woodruffe-Peacock

The waiting room and facilities at Immingham Dock station with a precast concrete bay for the station's coal in the foreground.

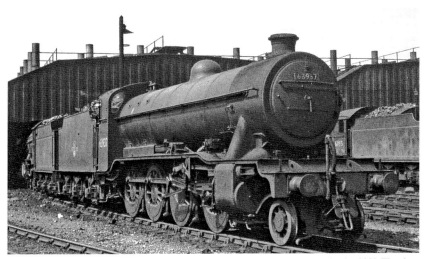

Gresley class 02/2 3 cylinder 2-8-0 No 63937 of Retford shed at Immingham shed in May 1961. The class 02/2 engines were introduced in 1924 as a development of Gresley's GNR 02 2-8-0s and as can be seen they retained their GNR style of cab. *J. Davenport*

An iron-ore train double-headed by class 37s Nos 37351 and 37377, comes off the Immingham line and moves past the ornate Brocklesby station en-route to Scunthorpe on 2nd May, 1990. *R. Manning*

Class V2 2-6-2 No 4771 'Green Arrow' on the Grimsby Immingham Light Railway approaching Woad Lane level crossing Great Coates, heading towards Immingham on The Great Central railtour on the 3rd of March 2007. *W. Gladwell*

BR standard class 9F 2-10-0 No 92039 close to Immingham coal plant in May 1960. Put into traffic in December 1954 No 92039 had two spells at Immingham from February 1959 until September 1962 and from November 1963 until June 1964. It was withdrawn in October 1965.

In this view from the west in October 1991 we can see the old engine shed to the left and the new diesel maintenance shed to the right. *D. Enefer*

BARTON & IMMINGHAM LIGHT RAILWAY

In order to bring New Holland traffic to lmmingham, the Barton & Immingham Light Railway was constructed and opened in two stages. The first, from Immingham West Junction to Killingholme came into use on 1st December, 1910, while the second, to a junction with the Grimsby to New Holland line at Goxhill, was opened on 1st May, 1911. The title of the railway is deceptive in that the proposed section between Goxhill and Barton-on-Humber was never built. The track between Immingham and Goxhill was single throughout, with tiny intermediate halts at Killingholme and East Halton. Passenger services between New Holland and Immingham began operating on 2nd May, 1911.

The very basic facilities provided at East Halton Halt on 28th April, 1954. The drabness somewhat relieved by the presence of an attractive seat and two lamp standards. *H. C. Casserley*

BARTON & IMMINGHAM LIGHT RAILWAY.

On MONDAY, 1st MAY, 1911,

THE NEW RAILWAY

Between

GOXHILL&IMMINGHAM

will be opened and a Service of Trains
will run as under:—

WEEK DAYS.

	a.m. 5 20A	a.m. 8 25	a.m. 11 50	p.m. 1 30	p.m. 5 20	p.m. 6 30
Hull (Corporation Pier) dep.	5 20A	8 25	11 50	1 30	5 20	6 30
New Holland ....arr.	5 40	8 45	12 10	1 50	5 40	6 50
Barton-on-Humber...dep.	...	8 20	11 40	1 0	5 15	6 35
New Holland .... ,,	5 45	8 50	12 15	1 55	5 45	7 0
Goxhill ......,............... ,,	5 50	8 55	12 20	2 0	5 50	7 5
East Halton .... ,,	5 58A	9 3	12 28	2 8	5 58	7 13
Killingholme................... ,,	6 4A	9 9	12 34	2 14	6 4	7 19
Immingham ....arr. (Western Jetty)	6 10	9 15	12 40	2 20	6 10	7 25

	a.m. 6 15	a.m. 10 0	B p.m. 12 50	B p.m. 3 15	B p.m. 6 23	B p.m. 8 40
Immingham ....dep. (Western Jetty)	6 15	10 0	12 50	3 15	6 23	8 40
Killingholme ....· ,,	6 21	10 6	12 56	3 21	6 29	8 46
East Halton .... ,,	6 27	10 12	1 2	3 27	5 35	8 52
Goxhill .... ,,	6 35	10 20	1 10	3 35	6 43	9 0
New Holland ....arr.	6 40	10 25	1 15	3 40	6 48	9 6
Barton-on-Humber... ,,	7 35	11 5	1 35	4*46	7 37	9 20
New Holland ....dep.	6 45	10 48	1 20	3 45	7 5	9 15
Hull (Corporation Pier) arr.	7 5	11 8	1 40	4 5	7 25	9 35

* Thursdays only.

WORKMEN'S WEEKLY RETURN TICKETS

will be issued to **IMMINGHAM** (Western Jetty) by trains marked **A**,
available for return by trains marked **B**, at the following fares:—

	s. d.		s. d.
Hull (C.P.)	**2 6**	**East Halton** ...	**1 0**
	Killingholme ...	**6d.**	

Marylebone Station,
London; April, 1911.   BY ORDER.

Knapp, Drewett & Sons Ltd., 30, Victoria Street, Westminster, and Kingston-on-Thames.—G.C. 1214.

HEATH ROBINSON OUTDONE

Despite the high technology employed in the building of the new port it was a very different kind of technology which caught the eye of "Perambulator", writing in the 1920s. He had set out to walk the 14 miles from Riby to New Holland but found himself instead at Immingham. "The journey I took was via Habrough station. Here the stationmaster was most enthusiastic about his trains and their convenience and reliability. He boasted of the amazing cheapness of the tickets, the purchase of which would entitle me to be carried to Hull for just 1s 7d return. And so to Immingham Dock, meeting railwaymen who were sure I would not be allowed to go much further without being arrested or at least turned back. Then, at last, the peace and quiet of the railway sidings, with their miles of track and thousands of trucks.

At last to the platform of West Dock Station. Having an hour to wait for my train I left the station and crossed a lock bridge from where the electric trams start for Grimsby. Hardly had I got over the water when the bridge was opened for a ship to pass, and it remained open. There

A GCR motor-train at Barton-on-Humber at the turn of the twentieth century. Barton was the terminal of a short branch line from New Holland. Today it is an interchange between a rail service from Grimsby and a bus connection to Hull via the Humber Bridge.

was I, much less than an hour before train time, on the wrong side of the water and no sign anywhere of any intention to close the bridge again. Five o' clock and only twenty minutes to the train. At that moment I saw an amazing Heath Robinson contraption float slowly into view on the other side of the dock, a black barge with a high wooden causeway rigged along the top of it. At each end was a collection of ropes, pulleys and cogwheels and swinging gangways. The barge was moored into position and made fast between the two sides of the dock.

A naval officer tugged at the ropes and bits of wire. In so doing he coaxed and lowered pieces of wood and lengths of boarding until there appeared from each end of the floating barge what was a genuine Heath Robinson bridge. This was obviously for travellers like myself, who found themselves on the wrong side of Immingham Dock and were in agonies of fear that they were going to miss their train.

Over the bridge I came, not daring to laugh, as the officer was watching me, but once on solid earth, with nothing between me and my train, I shook with delight and turned for one last look at that marvel of pulleys and ropes".

The boat train on Eastern Jetty is seen from the deck of a visiting liner. The coach at the rear of the train is East Coast Main Line clerestory stock T. Harden

MIDNIGHT SUN CRUISES

During the 1920s and 30s the Orient Line ran "Midnight Sun Cruises" from the Eastern Jetty, attracting passengers from all over the country. The Orient Line specials always created a stir at the dock. The Appendix to the Rule Book ran, "During the period from 20 minutes before the time of arrival of the first Special and the arrival of the second at Immingham Dock, and from 20 minutes before the booked time of departure of the first Special and until the second Special has cleared Immingham East Junction, no engine other than the Special train engines must be permitted to pass between East Junction and Transit Sheds, or foul the lines over which the Specials will run".

The following refer to trains running to and from Immingham in July 1939. Train No 249 conveyed dining car stores from Marylebone and Neasden Sidings and arrived at 9.20 am. The next train No 250, was first class only and left Neasden Sidings at 10.20 am. It was made up of ten coaches, plus restaurant cars. Upon leaving Marylebone at 11.48 am, it called at Rugby, Leicester, Nottingham Victoria, then ran via Tuxford, calling at Pyewipe Junction at 3.31 pm for water and arrived at Immingham Dock at 4.41 pm.

Train No 251 was a composite, with the engine running light engine, tender first, from Ardwick to Manchester Central, arriving at 1.43 pm. The train departed at 2.10 pm and was made up of eight coaches, plus a restaurant car and a large parcel van next to the engine. It called at Guide Bridge, Penistone and Sheffield Victoria at 3.32 pm, where a through carriage from the 1.18 pm ex-Liverpool Central was attached to the rear. Travelling via Retford the train arrived at Immingham at 5.35 pm.

The first of the return specials, Nos 253 and 254, left Immingham at 9.25 am for Marylebone. These trains were routed via Waleswood and arrived in London at 2.48 pm and 3.09 pm respectively. The Manchester train left Immingham at 10.25 am and arrived at 1.48 pm.

A scene inside the shed at Immingham depot Open Day on 1st September, 1974. *P. Haith / D. Enefer*

Two unidentified class B1 4-6-0s and a class 9F 2-10-0 inside Immingham shed.

ENGINE SHED

Built in the south eastern corner of the dock estate, Immingham Shed (40B) opened in 1912 and at its peak had an allotment of over 120 locomotives. It closed to steam in February 1966, by which time it had become one of the last depots on the Eastern Region  to boast a steam allocation. The last steam locomotive to work from the shed was class B1 4-6-0 No 61058, with a train of empty wagons for Markham Colliery, on 7th February, 1966.

The shed was built to house a large fleet of locomotives required to service the new dock and the copious amount of traffic guaranteed by the docks here and at Grimsby. A large coaling stall was built along the northern side of the shed, a mechanical coaling plant was introduced at the western end of the LNER in the 1930s. Two 65ft turntables were installed – one at the eastern end of the depot, the other at the eastern end of the reception sidings.

Part of the original building was demolished in the mid-1960s to make way for a new diesel depot. It was opened in 1966, south east of the steam shed, which was converted to a wagon repairing facility. The new depot was 78ft x 367ft. In 1966 its allocation was 90 diesels and 35 shunters.

At an open-day at Immingham Depot in September, 1974, the following locomotives were on display: Class 55 Deltic; Class 47 Brush/Sulzer; Class 37 English Electric; Class 31 Brush Type 2; Class 20 English Electric; Class 76 Electric locomotive used on the Manchester-Sheffield-Wath route and a Trans-Pennine Diesel Multiple Unit.

A total of 325 staff were employed at the depot, including 170 footplatemen and 125 workshop staff responsible for locomotive and wagon maintenance.

Following the splitting up of the former BR Trainload business into three companies in 1994, the depot came under the brief control of Loadhaul, which was acquired and merged into English, Welsh & Scottish Railways (EWS) in 1995. As a result of the centralization of maintenance activities by EWS, the depot was only used as a fueling point and for the storage of out-of-service locomotives.

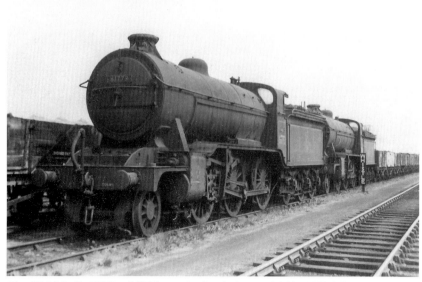

Class K2 2-6-0s No 61773 and 61756 stored at Immingham on 8th May, 1960. *D. Enefer*

Robinson GCR class 8J (NER class C4) 4-4-2 No 2918 in the company of a class 04 2-8-0. Many of the graceful Robinson Atlantics worked out their last years of service from this shed on local passenger work. Despite the patina of neglect and black LNER livery its not difficult to see why these curvaceous engines acquired the name 'Jersey Lilies'.

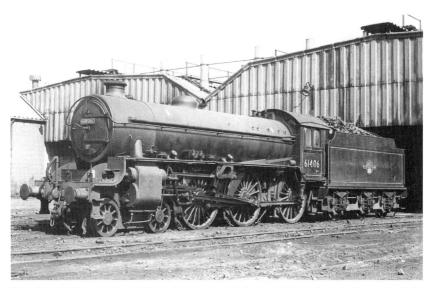

Class B1 4-6-0 No 61406 of 40B Immingham shed in August 1965. Built at Darlington in 1950, No 61406 had a brief working life, being withdrawn in April 1966. *Real Photographs*

Class B1 4-6-0 No 61360 runs alongside Immingham shed in October 1965. The new diesel depot is being built behind the engine. *M Black*

Immingham-based Cowan Sheldon steam crane lifting the water tank near Kirton-in-Lindsey tunnel. The breakdown train was used over a wide area bounded by Cleethorpes, Louth, Sleaford and Scunthorpe. *Immingham Museum*

Class WD 2-8-0 No 90480 at Immingham shed. *Immingham Museum*

Class B1 4-6-0 No 61379 'Mayflower' at Immingham on 8th May, 1960. It was the only one of its class to be named after the 1948 nationalisation of the railways. It had plaques fitted to its cab side in 1952 which read "This locomotive was named 'Mayflower' on 13th July, 1951, as a symbol of the ties between the two towns of Boston and the long friendship between the USA and the British Commonwealth". One of its nameplates now resides in Boston, Lincolnshire, the other in the USA. *D. Enefer*

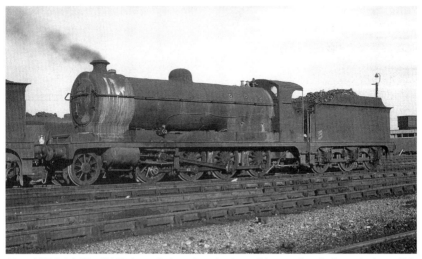

Class O4/7 2-8-0 No 63644, in typical work stained condition, at Immingham shed on 18th September, 1960. It was rebuilt to part 7 in 1943 with a Gresley boiler. *N. Glover*

The dormitory at Immingham shed, known as 'The Barracks'. One can understand why engine crews from the bustling city of Manchester did not enjoy staying at this isolated place.

An inspector and shunting staff pose in front of one of Immingham's Class 08 0-6-0 diesel shunters at **Brick Pit Sidings.** *Immingham Museum*

'THE BARRACKS'

Soon after the opening of the shed a dormitory block was built alongside the depot turntable. This building was provided because the small village of Immingham was some distance from the engine shed; Grimsby was too far away for engine crews to lodge when bringing trains to Immingham from other depots. The Immingham dormitory quickly became known as "The Barracks" by train crews. The new building was eloquently described in the "GCR Journal" of February 1915. "The provision of dormitories was inaugurated by the GCR at Gorton, with a building exclusively for drivers and firemen. The arrangements met with such appreciation that similar accommodation was subsequently provided at Sheffield, Immingham, Lincoln and Woodford.

The caretaker residence is attached to one end of the main building and contains a sitting room, two bedrooms and a bathroom for the private use of the caretaker and his wife. When a driver, fireman and guard leave duty at Immingham shed, his inspector or foreman supplied them with a permit admitting them to the dormitory. On the permit is entered the time he leaves duty and the time he requires to be called for duty again.

On entering the dormitory each man hands his permit to the caretaker, who allots him a bedroom and writes his name on a large board with the number of the room and the time he needs to be called. After registering the men are at liberty to use the lavatories and the bathroom. In the dining room, should they follow the almost invariable custom of cooking their own meals, they will find a range of kettles, pans and crockery.

On the opposite side of the hall is the recreation room, equipped with small tables and games, such as draughts and dominoes, as well as the daily papers. Smoking is permitted in the dining and reading rooms but prohibited elsewhere in the building.

From the hall on the ground floor and the landing on the first floor swing-doors give access to the dormitories. Here arranged on two floors are 39 cubicles each provided with a comfortable bed and clean linen. In addition to the cheerful open fires in the dining and reading rooms, the building is heated by radiators. The charge made for the accommodation is 1/- per lodge."

Class N5 0-6-2T No 69305 works a short goods train at Immingham in the 1950s. *C. T. Goode*

Visiting ex-LMS class 5 4-6-0 No 44861 beside the water column at the east end of Immingham shed on 8th November, 1964. *W. Gladwell*

WD 'Austerity' 2-8-0 No 90221 with class 9F 2-10-0 No 92184 and 'Austerity' No 90055, all withdrawn, at the rear of 40B on 21 March, 1965. In the rear can be seen the coaling stage, the water tank and water softening plant. *W. Gladwell*

Class Y3 Sentinel shunter 0-4-0 No 68162 at Immingham in May 1950. Immingham Sentinels worked fish offal, in special vehicles with sliding doors to minimise the smell, between Grimsby Fish Docks and the offal factory at Killingholme. They also moved tank wagons between the oil terminal at Killingholme and Immingham Western Jetty. Built in September 1930, withdrawn from running stock in January 1956 it entered Departmental stock as No 21 in March 1956 and was scrapped in July 1960. *Real Photographs*

Bernard Bontoft stands alongside WD 2-8-0 No 90075 which was shedded at Immingham in 1950 and is seen in its familiar work-stained condition. *Immingham Museum*

Class B1 4-6-0 No 61213 leaves New Holland with a passenger train for Cleethorpes on Friday 1st October, 1954. *A. C. Ingram*

Ex GCR class J11 0-6-0 No 64284 stands in front of a class 04 2-8-0 near the coaling tower at Immingham. The white smokebox door hinge was characteristic of Immingham shed. No 64284 was noted in the New Holland Town Station Occurrence Book as having "failed" there on 19th January, 1951. *N. E. Stead*

Immingham shed roof was replaced with a corrugated asbestos one supported on a lightweight steel framework. In this 1960s view the allocation consisted of ex-LNER and Standard Class locomotives. *W. T. Stubbs*

A class J94 0-6-0ST and a brake-van on No 16 pilot duties, heading for Grimsby East Marsh. No 16 worked between West Marsh, West Bank across the Royal Dock swing bridge to East Marsh, also GNR goods yard at Pasture Street and New Clee sidings. *Immingham Museum*

The LNER class J94 were ideal for shunting dock sidings being powerful and having a short wheelbase. On 6th September, 1947, No 8076 is seen during a pause in shunting box vans and wagons at Immingham. No 8076 was purchased by the LNER from the Ministry of Supply in 1946 and would, in due course, became BR No 68076, remaining in traffic until September 1960. *V. R. Webster*

IMMINGHAM TURNS

Two of the more interesting turns worked by Immingham engine crews were what became known as the "Eason's Specials" and the Manchester fish workings. The "Eason's Specials" were organised by the Grimsby travel agents of the same name. They ran on Thursdays and Saturdays and left Grimsby at 7.00 am and arrived at Kings Cross at 10.30 am. The return workings left Kings Cross at Midnight allowing passengers an afternoon and evening in London.

Prior to 1923 the trips were organised by the GNR and were a huge success. The newly-formed LNER regarded the arrangements for the excursions less than satisfactory. The bringing of engines and stock from Peterborough, New England, to operate the trips seemed to them to involve a lot of unnecessary running, particular as Immingham shed was only five miles from Grimsby.

Under the new arrangements Immingham men and engines were booked to work through to Kings Cross, where the men would lodge overnight. Sid Cleaver and Bill Croft learnt the road, the idea being that they would work alternate shifts. The first ever working of a GCR engine from Immingham to Kings Cross was on Saturday 29th September, 1923, with class B3 4-6-0 No 6169 "Lord Farringdon" in charge. The engine had recently being overhauled at Gorton and no doubt given extra attention at Immingham, to make a maximum impact at what had been the headquarters of the opposition, the GNR.

Class B3 No 6167 "Lloyd George" was also at Immingham at this time, bringing the numbers of the class to three. Two ex-GCR class 8C (LNER class B1 4-6-0) Nos 5195, and 5196 also worked the London trains.

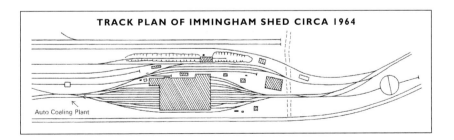

TRACK PLAN OF IMMINGHAM SHED CIRCA 1964

Auto Coaling Plant

The B1s and B3s were replaced by a trio of class B7 4-6-0s Nos 5469, 5482 and 5484 and these proved to be perfect engines for the job. In May 1933 class B2 No 5426 "City of Chester" arrived at Immingham, followed by No 5425 "City of Manchester" and 5423 "Sir Sam Fay" in June. No 5428 "City of Liverpool" followed in July and all were used on the London trains. The B3 class returned to Immingham in the shape of No 6164 "Earl Beatty" and No 6167 in April 1935. Robinson's B3s dominated the specials until the outbreak of World War 2.

As part of the reorganisation, after 1923, Immingham crews lost one of their top jobs - the express fish to London, which were taken over by New England shed. The 5.10 pm fish train from Grimsby Docks to Ashton Moss, however was handed over from Gorton to Immingham in the mid 1930s. The Manchester workings were the domain of the B7 4-6-0s with Nos 5467, 5476, 5477 and 5478 all based at Immingham.

The Manchester workings began on Monday afternoon with the first of two crews signing on at Immingham at 2.45 pm and preparing their engine. At 3.45 pm they set off tender-first for New Clee Sidings, in Grimsby. By 4.45 pm they often had the maximum of 45 wagons behind them ready for the off. There was a stop at Doncaster Marshgate for remarshalling. Vehicles for the Cheshire Lines Committee were taken off at Godley and further vehicles removed at Guide Bridge. The rest continued to Ashton Moss, where they were handed over to the LMS. The Immingham crew was relieved at Guide Bridge by Gorton men, and then walked to Gorton Barracks where they spent the night.

For the return trip the men booked on at 2.30 pm. They moved their engine a few hundred yards to Ashburys Yard to pick-up the 3.00 pm Ashburys-Grimsby Class "A" goods, which eventually reached Grimsby at 1.00 am. As the Immingham crew boarded their engine at Gorton the second crew was coming on duty to perform the Tuesday to Wednesday working.

The original Monday crew reappeared at Gorton on Friday night. The Ashburys-Grimsby train did not run on Saturdays. The men remained at Gorton overnight, taking out the 1.30 am newspaper and mails express to Cleethorpes. They came on duty at 12.55 pm on Saturday night so that the Company could class it as a Saturday working and avoid paying Sunday overtime rates!

D6746 on the fueling line at Immingham shed. *Immingham Museum*

British Railways standard class 9F 2-10-0 No 92037 with 'Vote Labour' chalked on its cylinder cover, on shed at Immingham on 27th December, 1964. Brought into traffic in December 1954, 92037's short working life was brought to an end in June 1965 when it was cut-up at Drapers in Hull. *W. Gladwell*

D6964 derailed at Immingham being jacked and packed back into the running line. *Immingham Museum*

THE PRESENT DAY

With over forty sailings a week to Europe and Scandinavia and a deep-sea liner terminal serving worldwide destinations Immingham is a major port. Its roll-on roll-off services a huge success.

A significant part of its business is generated by the giant steelworks at nearby Scunthorpe. Large grain and fertilizer cargoes speak of the ports location in a rural agricultural region.

About 20% of the United Kingdom's oil refining capacity is adjacent to the port, which, together with a cluster of world-renown chemical companies along the Humber bank, generates large volumes of liquid bulk through four specialised terminals. To cope with the increase in size of some of the vessels the first phase of a new deep-water facility, the Humber International Terminal, became operational in June 2000, offering the only multi-purpose facility of its kind on the east coast between the River Thames and the Tees.

Instead of exporting vast amounts of coal Immingham now imports coal for industry and domestic use, most of which is still moved by rail. Significant amounts of steel products, timber, petroleum, chemicals and iron ore are also moved by trains. From Immingham Bulk Terminal twenty-six block trains of iron ore and coal leave daily for Scunthorpe steelworks.

Over four million tons of rail cargo annually leaves Lindsey Oil Refinery and Humber Oil Refinery, with twelve to fifteen block trains daily serving various destinations. The DFDS Nordic Terminal sees a million tons of mainly steel, chemical and forest products handled annually. In 2000 a total of 204,000 tons of export steel were moved from road to rail and transported from UK steel mills to customers on the Continent and Scandinavia.

Rising road costs and environmental concerns have put a new focus on railways, and total flexibility means it is no longer necessary to have full trainloads to reap the benefits. Incomplete loads are moved from Immingham to Doncaster where the freight traffic is re-marshalled into block trains for trunk services. Immingham remains one of the United Kingdom's leading ports for rail freight. The legacy of the Great Central Railway still endures today.

Immingham shed, in all its former glory, can be visited in model form at Immingham Museum, on the corner of Pelham Road and Washdyke Lane, on Wednesday to Saturday afternoons. We are very grateful for the help they have given us in the preparation of this book.

The men of Immingham

Mr Kirkman, the running foreman.

Ron Connell aboard a B1.

Ron Drake, Bill Harboard, Jim Seed
and Rolly Harrison.

The yard staff take a break.

Fireman Ron Connell at
Gas House Sidings, Cleethorpes.

A group of railwaymen put the world
to rights.